Sean O'Brien's eleven collections of poetry include *The Drowned Book* (2007), *Europa* (2018) and *It Says Here* (2020). His work has received awards including the T.S. Eliot Prize, the Forward Prize, the E.M. Forster Award, and most recently the 2020 Beijing Literature and Arts Network Award for Poetry for lifetime achievement. His other work includes fiction, drama, criticism and translation. In 2020 his translation of the *Collected Poems* of the Kazakh national poet Abai Kunanbayuli was published, and in 2021 he edited Alistair Elliot's *This is the Life: Selected Poems*. His poems have been widely translated. He is Emeritus Professor of Creative Writing at Newcastle University and a Fellow of the Royal Society of Literature. He lives in Newcastle upon Tyne.

Sean O'Brien

Embark

PICADOR

First published 2022 by Picador
an imprint of Pan Macmillan
6 Briset Street, London EC1M 5NR
EU representative: Macmillan Publishers Ireland Ltd,
Macmillan Publishers Ireland Limited, 1st Floor, The Liffey Trust Centre,
117–126 Sheriff Street Upper, Dublin 1 D01 YC43
Associated companies throughout the world
www.panmacmillan.com

ISBN 978-1-5290-9685-9

1 3 5 7 9 8 6 4 2

A CIP catalogue record for this book is available from the British Library.

Printed and bound by TJ Books Ltd, Padstow, Cornwall PL28 8RW

Visit **www.picador.com** to read more about all our books
and to buy them. You will also find features, author interviews and
news of any author events, and you can sign up for e-newsletters
so that you're always first to hear about our new releases.

In memory of Birtley Aris

Contents

Embark

The Desks

I dream of how, when we have gone, the city turns
to introspection, seeking themes and patterns
from innumerable instances. Where to begin?
Why not the dank accommodation shadows reach
beneath a railway arch, or better still, the stairs descending
past the nearby offices of lawyers and comedians,
deeper than the scope of public scrutiny –
the sort of thing I'd choose, if I existed –
ending in a place, if that is what it is,
where no attempt at decoration has been made,
with one anachronistic admonition
bolted to the wall, concerning boiler-ash,
and next to that a single door, too wide, too low,
that opens on a chamber whose far end is not shown,
at which innumerable desks and chairs are aimed,
awaiting God knows what examination.

Furniture

Should I ring or knock or walk straight through the open door
and up the stairs of your old house
to pick my way among the shifting population
of your recent acquisitions,
chairs and cupboards, dressers, hat-stands
jostling like the broker's men along the landing?
Though you can always see the humour in the omen,
lighting up inside the smell of ancient smoke,
will I find you staring at your latest wardrobe,
parked so that it blocks the window bay
and throws its shadow on your mirrored face?

The house is sold, the furniture dispersed
into the auctioneers' where you unearthed it,
and there is no you to visit, no way back
to those incendiary curls, the shy and difficult
princess of Ireland, sequestered and interred
among her monumental odds and ends.
I know the exit to the underworld
lies somewhere here, on Spring Bank West
before the restoration, in behind the downcast angels
and the ivy and the columns lagged with moss.
I know this place I've never seen, and so must you.

The sky is gone. The trees, the birds, the waterfall
and we ourselves are stone. At leisure on a stone divan,
among the yawning wardrobes and the mirrors
in obsidian, the names and dates incised
on every surface in reverse, while smoke
continues rising from a grate of stone,
we must be getting warm, but Hell will neither wait
nor long for us: it has forgotten what it never knew,
your woolly yellow tights, the bird-beat of your heart
as you lay sleepless in my arms,
the marble wing of madness poised above your head.

Wine-glasses

'Sie, wie unsre Schalen sich durchdringen
ohne Klirrn.'

Rilke, 'Vase Painting'

The wineglasses move through each other
in silence, not touching. The wine
flows into itself and away.
Slow spending of the world
against the clock. Aren't we a pair?
Why do I feel required to approve?

They still exist, those empty rooms
where we passed through one another
night by night. The rose
in the wineglass, the rose in the mirror,
left there on the mantelpiece, remains
a rose. It was not of my choosing.

No matter. But approve of what?
These insubstantial bodies falling
through and through the absence of forever?

So be it. Let me raise a glass to you
as in another room you raise your own,
to set the silence ringing as we go.

An Arch Wherethro'

The ingénue is waiting in the wings,
Concealed among the jasmine's snowy stars.

One year in ten they flower. Beyond the arch
A group of patched-up sheds implies

A further world, and there perhaps
A version of the pastoral identical to ours

Takes place upon a grassy stage
Among a rich man's flowering lawns –

Love-play; reversal; the unmasking;
Songs to finish. Comedy. And yet

Milord does not attend. So everything
That furnishes a private age

With charm and mystery, dew and sweat,
Must be and save itself as best it can –

The goddess waits and waits. Where is the cue?
Red-black smoke-bush, downcast ferns,

A fungus like a sulphur toad, and spiders
Singing at their silver work: all these

Possess themselves in patience
Unto death, which is content. And yet –

Keep Out

The wood belongs there. But the tumbled wall
And the iron gates long since unhinged
Would have you think that the estate itself
Was never new, that here is the original

Whose copper beech and monstrous laurels
Were the servants of the grand design
Of everything this silence means to say:
Keep out, keep out, desire not.

Which must be why we come at dusk.
Although the keeper's dead and gone,
To trespass in this senile paradise
Might still incur a penalty, a tax perhaps

On understanding, so that when we disbelievers
Wander in, the danger is that we may feel
We 'understand' the longing that secured
Itself against the likes of us, and in this way

Become the dead who long for heaven too,
But only to possess it, like the damned.

The Rose-Giver

The one lady owner of all you see,
Receive a further rose from me,
Bearing carefully in mind
This latest bloom must also serve
As notice that I have resigned.

It would be foolish to suppose
That there will always be a rose
To flatter your imperious whim.
The lover and the lowest slave
Must seek their pleasures in the grave.

If from that grave – as no one knows –
There should uncoil a pure black rose,
The shade of your unnatural heart
And outcome of unnatural art,
Best not to wish for one of those.

Address Unknown

They're irrevocable, of course,
the damp distempered rooms
that have not thought of you
in fifty years. But dust-motes
are still slowly dancing
in the gap between the curtains
someone's hopeful mother
ran up to surprise you with.

And here's a glass abandoned
on a marble mantelpiece
to die of thirst. The mirror's
been unscrewed and sold
despite its provenance, and next
we find a pair of stockings
hanging in the bathroom.
Looks like quite a party.

Knowing nothing, you are still
an eye, as empty as the skylight
staring down the barrel
of that staircase, where the girls
to whom you introduced themselves
would sit and weep, then,
gathering their things, forget you
carefully, with any luck.

The Undertaking

Last of the futurists,
the undertakers listen carefully.

First rain, then influenza.

*

Look, it's forty years ago,

sex and drugs and literary criticism –
heady stuff in the tall white rooms

half a generation dreams of still,
between the Calor heater

and the streaming windows,
where the poetasters brandished

their pathetic fallacies. The girls
were learning to make do and leave.

It is over. It scarcely began.
The faces in the ecstasies

of smudged mascara still lie
sealed inside the mirror,

and the poets who were mainly
men but scarcely that remember

as they drink. *Maudits, we were
abandoned by those bitches. Ai!*

*

These days the women cannot tell
when this sick-visiting began

and do not like to dwell
on where it ends. Ding dong.

At times like these the undertaker
seems to be your only friend.

'76

The heat. The ageing boys play football in the park
as a reprieve from skinning up.
The girls with their endless summer legs
wait underneath the limes, then wander off
towards the shops, to try on necklaces
and run their fingers over silk. There must be
something else, eventually. Back on the street
they shield their eyes against the glare
and look about as if it should be obvious.
         It's three o'clock. And then it's five.
Still the heatwave does not break.
The shut-up glasshouse sweats green shadows
and the air is dancing on the grass.
When the girls return with carriers of beer
the ball is nowhere to be seen. The boys
are lying in the sun, half-stripped
like dead hussars. The flies have triumphed.
         Evening falls, and smoke goes curling
round the curtains and away into the blue.
The girls are sewing buttons back
on threadbare velvet trousers.
The water-clock ticks on downstairs
and up here everything's inflammable,
so who loves who, and in what order?
And how long will it require
to exhaust the permutations
and attain the parched, indifferent

extremity that one or two of these
alleged voluptuaries have read about?
            And afterwards? No afterwards,
or none that history records.
For them the war was over. Born to live
beyond their means, to be what
all the boring unknown past was aiming at,
they never cared to notice
they were out of fashion and excuses.
Nowadays the names escape me
but I see them still, far off across the park,
last of their kind, a ragged royalty, pretenders
to a dying sun, awash with lazy fires.

Formalities

Exhausted mercury, its shine long lost,
the grey blood thickens in the heart.
I am this poison. There remains no art
to spare us what must happen last.

One chamber empties: does the other fill,
or is this all a pause that's no such thing?
The body fails to answer to the will.
No time. No time. No more malingering.

At once fantastic and banal, the fact
accelerates away, and there I go,
no wiser, lacking what I always lacked:

so let thermometers and scalpels show
that I and I alone was the disease,
and make an end of these formalities.

The Runners

The elegant women who run with their dogs
through the graveyard, where have they been before now?
They are so self-possessed, yet too preoccupied
with elsewhere and with afterwards to be
entirely present. To be forty-odd and run like that
seems close to immortality. They glide on
through the sunlit pools between the lime-trees,
down to where the tunnelled shade begins
among the older tombs with ironwork
and obelisks and disregarded claims
to time's attention. There they pause
to take a call, or block one. They must have it
all to do, like emissaries
from a new creation, one that like our own
is taken up with its supreme particulars.
I wish that we could be each other's witnesses,
as if I were the past for you, as you for me,
the moment when the cherry-tree
unsleeves its ice-pink trumpery
and turns to dying, while the blackbirds pick
dispassionately among the stones
to pass the time, as though this morning's
not the thing itself, the first hot day,
but instead a late revision of the future
playing out in real time, able to predict
our chances to the second,
only somehow set aside, like good advice

that in the moment of its giving
wears its welcome out. I see you
pause before the tunnel's mouth, your phones
aloft like torches, and I see your dogs,
so loving and so eager for the off,
and now you see them too and smile
and glide away into the dark.

＊

A Last Turn

'Take a last turn | in the tang of possibility.'
Seamus Heaney, 'Linen Town'

This early in the morning it appears
a public square is most itself
when empty, standing in

for all the lost arrondissements,
the attics where we never met,
the empty index of the A to Z.

Rain is falling on the metal tables
piled with chairs, and gleaming
as it floods the blue brick gutters,

perfect and anonymous and beautiful.
Be careful what you wish for now
the very air has somewhere else to be.

The city has a headache
but it dare not speak its name –
the bitter patience that till yesterday

we learned from later middle age –
and now the plague is blown
as lightly as a kiss across the street.

Go home and bar the door. Seal up
the cracks with towels. Do it now,
when it is only just too late.

Discreetly

If they could only catch you for a moment
in a doorway on a corridor
when the symposium was over,
half in shadow – *still* no lightbulbs to be had –
they liked to call themselves
internal émigrés. They'd like it better still
if you would only say it too. *For was it not
the case*, they'd ask, that they alone
*had cared and risked enough
to give a life entirely
to work in solitude until such time
as the inferno had consumed itself?*
At which point they'd come blinking out,
stone-deaf with modesty,
into the sour, grainy light
where cities rose from ash
and bone and oven-stink
that overnight became discreet.
*Difficult days, you understand, the long
dark days, my friend*, the dry soul
watered with the tears of ink, *dry days*,
and yet with principles at least
to be upheld, as the legs uphold
a dumb piano covered in a dust-cloth
in that house where no one seemed to live,
the one that holds an air of occupation,
sweat and soap, bone soup and curdled time.

You know the kind of place I mean,
the air exhausted and the mantel-clock
like a recidivist, forgetting, then forgetting –
I was saying. But of course you were,
As corridors like this could testify.

Ever After

These things we hold to be self-evident:
the pigs will not perish nor the wolf repent,

and none will forgo or forget or forgive
since forever is where the wild things live.

Once upon a time, therefore, therefore,
the big bad wolf once more, once more

puts on his ancient stinking moleskin trousers
and goes out to blow down the little pigs' houses.

Rubies

for G

When I turn for home, in the street's black river
fish by Klee are frozen, rust and gold,

a shoal of earrings over which
the rowan-berries blaze, unfallen.

If the street is endless, yet the ice is coming,
how can both be true?

At your dressing-table
you are choosing earrings from the box

beside the ring-tree. Put back
the reticent amethyst

and let the far-off turquoise wait
in the midsummer dusk

at Heraklion. Choose rubies now,
with drops of gold, and wear them always.

Quinces

for Jo Reade

Eat what you're given and be grateful,
I was always told, then told again,
and I was grateful by the plateful,
but I was never ever given quinces.
I'm late to this mouth-music, rosy-gold,
vanilla-honey, sunlit distance . . .
tribute to the pagan senses –
although let me reassure you,
Aunties, Nana, Mum, that I was always
thankful for whatever I was given.
But nothing else has tasted so like heaven.
That wants eating, you would say,
but not by you, and not today.
Hands off. Besides, it's good to share.
Of course it is, but what if no one
knows the secret of these quinces
waiting for me in the larder?
You fed me with your principles, but look:
this case is altogether harder.
See these quinces? They won't last,
as Frost remarked of all things gold.
All I can offer you is words:
it follows then that self-denial

cannot but be self-defeating,
and yet I'll do as I was always told.
You hated waste. I'm grateful. So I'm eating.

Lord Back-End

The gabardine. The belt of twine. Brown paper
poking from the trouser-cuffs. Those rings
like knuckledusters, and the wand of bone that steers
an entourage of frosty air. You've been outflanked.
Now all fall down for Lord Back-End.
You that were gold shall be brought low
and you who governed dig your graves –
proverbial, it must be true –
the ring of pick-axes and spades on iron ground
is everywhere inside these woods.
Perhaps you haven't listened. See, a moment
seals the stream in ice upon a lip of stone.
Your moon-white face is there among the fish.
You must have missed the toadstools, then,
who having grown into themselves
like Arcimboldos of deformity
renounced this world and turned to slime.
And the crow falling out of the tree
in a bundle of rags, with no last words.
No hesitation. Doesn't bounce.
Lord Back-End sees, and it is good.
He pokes it with his stick. But as for you,
are you still here, and if so why?

Woodworks

for the chatelaine

Rooks
The sitting tenants of the hilltop
keep a weather eye on everything.
Oh, they've heard it all before.
Surprise us, they say. Go on. Thought not.

Leaf-storm
At dusk the woods are hurrying away,
clutching all they can carry –
time to be gone. It is over again –
except for the rowan, who stands
wearing only the gale and her earrings.

Ferns
Gamboge before brown
and then done to a crisp,

the ferns lie down, forgetting
summer. This is sleep,

it is sleep, says the goddess
passing through, her blue gown

pressed and cool and brisk
as any Englishwoman

taking charge at need. It is sleep
whose words are once more

ceasing to be words. Lie down
among the ferns now. Sleep.

Waterworks

Indifferent to sorrow as to time,
the rain is bouncing off the outhouse roof
to meet itself, for added emphasis.

If proof were needed, here is proof:
the sheer redundancy of days like this:
les très riches heures inside the glut of rhyme –

long days of impotent hyperbole and death,
dank-shadowed laurel-arch and dripping trellis,
while a mountainside collapses on a train

and we sit waiting for the minister to tell us
what's wrong now. We know he'll blame the rain
for raining and the poor for drawing breath,

but 'science shows' that we are the disease.
We cannot heal ourselves, nor wish to:
witness the pale rider writ in lemon juice

across the bottom of the contract, seen
only when you've put a match to it. Who knew
that all the M & Ms in Hell are brown?

The balsa mermaid in the bathroom
gazes with approval at her glass – it's been
brim-full forever but will never overbrim:

Unlike non-swimmers such as you and me,
she animates the world by being seen
at home in her *cathédrale engloutie*.

It's raining in the library too, a drizzle
made of dust and all the dreaming hours
we used to think we could embezzle

from the stern recording angel on the desk.
Now even she must wipe her specs and ask
what odds it makes to exercise her powers

or not. Though poems should not mean but be,
all information tends to entropy:
What was the Word is emptied of itself

and speechless water rises through the stacks,
engulfing like a continental shelf,
implacable as death or income tax.

Precipitation looms on every front.
Life, it appears, is quite impossible
as well as everything that is the case.

Poor pelting slums and summer palaces
alike endure the rain, convinced that this will
all be over soon, although it won't.

You style yourself an inner émigré,
sequestered till the whole thing goes away.
You spend your mornings burning loaves of bread

and then begin the reading you have planned
With Heraclitus and Chateaubriand,
till downtime, 'Box of Rain', the Grateful Dead.

At three a.m., when other people drown,
you're sick of Nemo's submarine romance.
You search the bathroom for a sleeping pill.

The mermaid turns to look at you askance:
where is the optimism of the will?
Go to your desk and drink your poison down.

Rain seethes like tinnitus inside the ear
and floods the chambers of the mind, as though
with hydra that will feast upon the brain

at leisure, but not kill it. You will undergo
an incomplete noyade, and you will hear
each time the creatures set to work again.

And do beware the demon of analogy
when casual similitudes invoke
the facts at which you merely meant to glance:

rain equals plagues and plagues R us. You wake
between the Devil and the deep blue sea
to find the nightmare real. You had your chance.

In Translation

When I was finally complete, the women saw straight through
me as I raised my hat. The snow fell like the sperm of angels on
the murky promenade. It seemed the women were all spoken
for by idiots who when in turn they raised their hats were my
doubles, a *mise en abîme* of bourgeois discontent, consumption,
syphilis and an appalling diet rich in salt and fat and alcohol.
Catholicism had not lapsed. Instead it crouched in endless
constipation. War had still not broken out. It was a privilege to
grasp all this, although I had no wish to be rewarded and still
less to die, which you surmise correctly

Poem in German

In these days of howling sunshine
when in the grove the aspens fret and pull
like maddened horses now silver now grey
in the curdling light, when the leaves of the cherry
are first all hands and then all birds
that point the way they cannot travel with you,
what then is to be done?

In the scrublands out by Benton Spur
where once allotments stood,
under the docks and the wheeling brambles
lies a pool, not much, but still, and there
you might at last donate your mineral content.
If the mine-cold water were not deaf
a passer-by might hear the shallow chink of bones
eventually. What else had you in mind?

Look – look – the wind is scouring the yellow grass,
the aspens may come down, and even if
as you still wish you could believe, all this
is simply a misunderstanding,
it will not be rectified. Can you not
feel the way your bones already sing
the pleasures of the pool to come,
the dissolution, liquid silence? What more could you ask?
The beautiful similes. Nothing avails.

Posterity

Friends, if we wait long enough
Our period charm may come around.
In the meantime let's get comfy,
Six feet underground.

Nemo Submerged

Inside the iron whale: the varnished ribs,
the drinking fountain and the orrery; inside,

O Captain, close as permanence can come,
in your *cathédrale engloutie*,

you draw the curtains on the bursting dark
where flailing monsters take their exercise.

Depth without pressure, cork-lined silence.
You have almost ceased to act, though still

you dress for dinner. Your moustache
is a philippic and your monocle glares white

with too much seeing, while you turn
another page of your redundant journal

and commit it to the stove. You ring the bell.
The ancient prisoners are admitted. *So, my friends,*

what news from the mouth-breathing upper world?
Say, Mr Land, if you've grown opposed

to cutlery, or still profess indifference?
Give us a tune. I'll burn your blue guitar to ash.

Of the Angel

The poor mad angel boy of twelve
With the unblinking gold-green stare
And the frightening permanent smile

That should be love but cannot be
Is brought by his mother to join the crowd.
Terrible as an army with banners

The girl cadets strike dulcimers
And the sounding brass of the Legion marches
Crisply on from 'Blaydon Races'

Via 'Who's Your Lady Friend?' and finally
Arrives at 'Tipperary' as they pass
Between the gates and down the cypress-glade

Towards the obelisk. There is a crowd in black
Among the graves, as if the resurrection
Is concluding just in time. Veterans, widows,

Idlers, dogs and babies. Is this everyone? Last Post.
The silence. Binyon's words. We undertake
'Abide with Me' but lack the heart for it

Under the vast incendiary light of the world,
The air still charged with fireworks,
Sun without pity, sky without end.

There is no home or resting place.
The broken ground will have us all
Indifferently back. And here he is,

Imprisoned in his element,
The angel boy who neither lives nor dies.
Where can his mother be? He waits among us,

Innocent and terrible. His smile is death,
And like the world his green-gold gaze
That should be love sees nothing everywhere.

Notes Towards a Supreme Afternoon

There is an afternoon where all the afternoons
Accumulate, like interest, you might say,
Though the account has been suspended
So that no reports or dividends are issued
Quarterly or annually or ever.
If as it were you had that kind of money,
What would such a sum secure? But even though
It's you who ask, one really couldn't say.
It would depend on all things being equal
And the sentiment prevailing on the day,
The bourse from which no traveller returns.
It could be nothing. It could be
Of sentimental value merely, and of that
Only you are competent to judge.
You see the difficulty, then? And yet
Were you to press now, were you to insist?
Although one does not care to speculate –
The smell of rain before it falls, perhaps,
Or burning leaves when there is fire
But no smoke, a kind of poetry, you might say,
Arriving neither late nor soon,
Of interest in an abstract kind of way,
Since nothing comes of it. But now
As you must also be aware, the clock's
Against us. Let us say good afternoon.

The Island

'Our end is life.'
Louis MacNeice, 'Thalassa'

Now Ariel has asked that he
Be re-admitted to the tree
And Caliban has spilt his seed
Along the desert shore,
And now that Prospero forgets
Whatever he was looking for,
And now the island, with no need
Of shipwreck or forgiveness,
Has no story left to tell,
When blind white noon and inky dark
Are neither here nor there
And love could hardly matter less,
Run out the boats. Embark, embark.

Song

Converting poetry to prose
they saw themselves as heaven-sent.
They tried to steal the compass rose.
They killed, since that was why they went,
and yet were hanged at Execution Dock.
For things are not as we suppose
and there is no man born as yet
to measure the divine estate.
West of the furthest west is set
a single adamantine gate
and on that gate a lock.
If this is all that history knows,
let the wise man burn his book,
and learning to possess his soul
in patience in his padlocked tomb
wait there beside the window-bars
to count the ticking of the clock
against the silence of the stars.

'No more poems about . . . foreign cities'

(Kingsley Amis)

No more foreign cities, then. We leave the archways
in the hidden lanes still waiting with their narratives of shade,

the meeting of two stairways at a nailed-up door,
the lives we almost put a name to.

Time, time is all we lacked, which is not true. We lacked
the inclination. Now the library of Sulaiman

is closed, not just on Thursday afternoons,
and all the elsewheres have been sent away, and now

the arches in their clouds of bougainvillea and jasmine
keep their counsel, stories not for wasting on a people

such as ours, who never learn and would not recognize
themselves in paradise or think it worth the journey.

Guide Michelin

Guide Michelin to Languedoc, I let you go
to charity, with all the maps,
because today there are no roads,
because the dust has settled after us
along the endless grove of limes
between the Aude and Ventenac, although
beneath the *Cave* the great canal
goes silently about its business
of reflection, on, on, between the willows.
Now the war is done, and what I think of it
like your advice and like your pointed silences
is neither here nor there –
likewise the scent of burning vines,
the blink of snow as pale as cataract
high up, beyond the plain, which as I say
it seems we crossed, although
I am forgetting – you and I, *Guide Michelin*,
when every road was setting out –

Stillness

A stillness comes when rain is imminent,
or when an insurrection you must never hear about
is crushed in a different part of the city.

Counting the days? How long can it be
since you could walk the teeming streets in idleness,
not minding if it rained, or if the police and military

sheltering beneath the colonnades seemed harder
day by day to tell apart? There was, you say,
a margin where you passed them by, and no one cared

and no one looked. That was the lifetime
you are struggling to reclaim – a girl in a blue dress
catching your eye, almost, in a dim bar-mirror? Perhaps.

A morning paper on a café table, melting
in the rain, perhaps. Her lateness, and the mess
of ordinary things? In any case, not now.

The rain is falling now. It takes no sides.
Like cherry-blossom falling in the square
before it has the time to die, the blood

that was not shed will wash away, and then,
supposing for a moment such things ever were,
it will be afterwards again, for good.

Correspondence

i.m. Peter Porter

The dead are faithful correspondents.
Your letters come out of the box
still talking, with their accent still in place,
their Mondays crowding to the window.
Here are books, jokes, an enemy's absurdity
and, in a wet spring in the Seventies,
Firenze, waiting for your scrutiny.
As you *said to the man in Niccolino's, there is
a shape to the world, more real than time,
more absolute than music.* Now you share it.
Let me hold this postcard up
against the black sun. The Queen of Heaven
and the Infant will endure the shade
and never know that this is death.

Swingbridgeman

My history is nobody's business.
To live here at all you must live here already.
I, boss, am the swingbridgeman
on the river that no one remembers.
Nowadays only gravel and corpses
come down from the bogs of beyond.
But if the city dreams at all, it dreams
of a bridge that might swing
once a month around midnight
when nobody's looking.
I tend the red light and the green
then after do myself a bacon fadge
and sit down to re-read Sven Hassel.
Pinned to the wall in 1953, Ava Gardner
and Lollobrigida give me the eye
when I study the runners and riders.
My skin is the grey of an eater of sulphur,
grey of the river of mud that flows under the river
and spends its leisure swallowing old barges.
Fuck knows why, sometimes I say
See me I'm Barmston Drain I am.
If ever I came to mind then folk
would think I'm long since done for.
But I deal in finer distinctions,
so that whilst I would instinctively
reject the metaphysical −
it's raining, visibility is poor, the whole place

smells of shit and death —
everything has led me to conclude
the place would have me for a god,
the oil-can and the drain-rod
brandished reassuringly aloft
and never mentioned yet relied on
hereabouts, which is the sum of things,
OK boss? Yours, the Swingbridgeman.

Not the Same

'Estuaries are not the same at all. They are neither one thing nor the other.'

Christopher Neve, *Unquiet Landscape*

One day you will meet yourself returning
over the mudflats, with your footprints disappearing
twice, first scoured off the sand by wind, then drunk
by mud whose unquenchable secret the sand preserves.
That day will resemble this, with the horizon
stricken from the record, and the sky likewise, although the sun
sinks heavy shafts of heat along the dunes as they dissolve.

Then what remains is sand and ochre, brown and yellow-grey,
while at the borders of the crusted banks, although the clock
is stopped, although the very mouth of time
seems choked with sand, although they are disqualified,
the little licking vortices of brackish water still intend to leave
or enter.
Here you are. The estuary is emptied of itself. There is no more.

Out in the three-mile mouth the tankers wait
beside the rusting fortress. Walking here and now
you trespass on a map that has unmade itself before
and taken back the island once adopted as it rose –
three miles of dead straight poplared road across the flats
that look like fields, the place all imitation,

Flemish, French, refrigerated by the sunken ages,
underwater still in all but name, Sunk Island,
which you cannot see.
                           You turn for home,
beneath the sudden vast discreet assembly
of the cumulus that stoops in from the west to gaze
at how the merest glass of water minus glass
revolving on an axis it alone can credit,
comes to meet itself repeatedly, to merge
and thus abandon its conceit, to glide
across the dried-out flats that have begun to glisten,
and where nothing quietly takes place.
With still air singing in your ears like shock,
and silence massing in the dimming rivermouth,
you should be long gone, cycling home,
or as the mind's eye wishes, lying swallowed in a trench
that water finds and claims and then forgets.

Stones

Under the snow, where the pub used to be,
a loathsome pond has settled down
on a bed of asbestos and pipework.
Here the stones are perfectly at home.

The little bastards live for this – the iron earth,
the plate-glass water like a vitrine
in 'a private collection'. Listen carefully
and you may hear them clench with joy.

No voices here. No opinions. The white field
narrow and long and unloved. Birds
at a pinch – one rook and one magpie

to set the thing off. Monochrome,
as stones apparently prefer. Think of them
rubbing their no-hands together. Job done.

A History

When frost and fog are gone to heaven
those far hills are far enough and more.

And yet, men say, still further off
the forests march against the Scots.

It is nobody's country.
                             When the rooks
perform their barebones offices

the flinty blackness of their chant
strikes sparks from the bitter air.

Wise to say nothing of fire or God.

While we are labouring, the sun
in all his arctic splendour

passes over, casting our shadows
like graves on the iron fields.

We're patched and nailed, got up
from dreams and hearsay, scraps of songs

and what this sudden solitary rider shouts
as he goes flying southward in the dusk.

Let Us Sit Down

So now what have you to say Anchises
nothing
        I can understand it
                I have carried you so long so deep
into the underworld that I am surely dead as you
and yet the plague is following to perpetuate the crisis

let me set you down and sit beside you now dear ghost
and while we wait I'll write another page
for all the spars and tackle that the sea has swallowed
for all the names of men and cities we have lost

for Carthage for the queen betrayed this heat this chill
and the incomprehensible instructions we have followed
to the letter
        is this it
            that we have crossed the blood-dark seas
to sit down with the dead at last at our infected ease

I used to think there was a point you had to make
by revelation or by anecdote or by sayings dark with meaning
but you could not articulate the thing you had in mind
and maybe that was it that in the end

there is really no such thing as higher learning
strive and seek oh all of that but what is there to find
except the fact
                the dead are dead
                                  is not enough
and though we are in Hell the cities go on burning

The Model-Maker

You began with the blood-red Supermarine
that won the Schneider Trophy. Its Platonic form
would make the Spitfire thinkable, I learn.
Mosquitoes followed, Stukas, Focke Wulfs
and Kawasaki Heins and Sturmoviks, the catalogues
of Frog and Revell and Aurora, soon replaced
with harder, better kits you sent away for,
destined to patrol the heavens of your room
and dive out of the sun to claim their kills.
Sprues like wreckage spread across your mother's table
in the prefab where the war was never done.
We came to tea and found an 88
embedded in a willow-grove, with field-grey figures
waiting to exist. What you discarded
I inherited, one company of Yanks and one of Krauts
in the imaginary Europe of the comic-books
where Jack Palance turned into Sgt. Rock
and every day would break out from St Lô.
My wars were dreams, but you took action –
endless time and glue and Humbrol. When I left
you were already laying down the Kriegsmarine
beside *Yamato* and *Repulse* and *Oklahoma*,
so that nothing should be lost except the crews.
You could create a blind white atoll, cured
by napalm, on the sea-road north to Okinawa,
or the field on Tinian where *Enola Gay* was armed.

Last man of a martial tribe, you lived to serve
but they would only have you at weekends.
What task remained, except to forge in miniature
a power neither questioned nor released
but imminent forever? You would take the Zero up
at first light, let the Kwaiten slip its moorings
at the Yasukuni temple, and unfurl the scarves
the girls of Hiroshima schools embroidered
to encourage death, then in that crimson dawn
the boy who plunged towards divinity would glimpse
the curvature of your imagined globe at last,
the view from nowhere gods alone enjoy.

From the Irish

i.m. SH and CC

where the blackbird at dawn
is still signing his name on the air
with a golden nib

The Reader, after Daumier

i.m. Alistair Elliot

If a train goes by, far off, there will be others.
This is the afternoon. It isn't over.
Light is falling through the green, becoming gold,
and as it alters once again makes light of you,
and you seem close to vanishing but never do.

The orchard where you sit and read
and wear that wide white umpire's hat
has made no plans, while *Phaethon*,
barely half a dozen lines of which survive,
completes itself between two pondered images.

The grandchildren will come and call you soon,
but soon does not arrive. This is, you wrote,
the life, the only life,
here between nowhere and never,
the fruit unfallen and the page uncut.

The Language

Falling through the aspen-grove
and ushering itself along the gutters, night rain
speaks a language you have never understood.

Where is the glossary that could admit
the drowning air and lustrous blackness
or the roaring? All this time

you have confused the subject with the method,
when the thing done is the thing itself
and not for keeping. The storm intensifies.

This dark is light enough to see the slick rain
shining on the slates like an effect
designed by God and yet no more designed

than all the nothingness your training
leads you to infer. Unsayable,
sipping at the rims of manhole covers

and revolving anti-clockwise
down a drainpipe for a laugh,
it runs off at the mouth, it drinks itself

and with its throat wide open
swallows, tasting nothing, neither noun
nor tense, insensibly particular,

oracular yet empty, pouring from the dark
into the dark, and still, for all his animated talk,
indifferently bearing Orpheus' head away.

Star of Bethlehem

i.m. Jacky Simms

Ornithogalum umbellatum

Your pilgrimage is halted here
beside the path, beneath the storm
that would uproot you:

far too few, and none to spare,
but times are evil: now the tiny
candour of your stars must be enough.

Acknowledgements

Agenda, Ambit, Bad Lilies, Butcher's Dog, Morning Star, New Boots and Pantisocracies, New England Poetry, New Humanist, One Hand Clapping, PN Review, Poetry London, Poetry Salzburg, Robert Graves Review, Stand, Ten Poems about History, The Irish Times, Times Literary Supplement.

'The Rose-Giver' appears in *His Thoughts More Green: Quatercentenary Poems for Andrew Marvell*, edited by David Wheatley, Broken Sleep Press, 2022.